D1308965

Salesforce1 Mobile App Admin Guide

Version 3, June 2015

Written by
Michelle Chapman-Thurber

With contributions by
Michael Floyd
Carol Franger
Tammy Rahn
Samantha Reynard
Emily Wilska

Note: Any unreleased services or features referenced in this or other press releases or public statements are not currently available and may not be delivered on time or at all. Customers who purchase our services should make their purchase decisions based upon features that are currently available.

This book is intended for administrators. With chapters on how to optimize your page layouts for mobile, customize the Salesforce1 navigation menu, create actions, work with compact layouts, set up mobile navigation, and much more, this book can help you get your organization ready for the Salesforce1 mobile experience.

Salesforce1 Mobile App Admin Guide

CONTENTS

Contents

CHAPTER 1   Introduction

The Salesforce1 mobile apps are mobile containers that enable you to experience all of the Salesforce App Cloud from any mobile device. The Salesforce1 mobile apps bring together Chatter, CRM, and business logic so you can connect to all of your data.

With the Salesforce1 mobile apps, your users can access custom objects and custom apps through the navigation menu and take advantage of custom actions to complete key tasks all from their mobile devices. Your users can also access their custom list views, receive notifications for posts and approvals that need their attention, get an immediate view of their day in the new "Today" app, or choose from a variety of mobile-optimized AppExchange apps to install.

Salesforce1 is fully customizable, allowing you to extend your custom apps to mobile using tools that you're already familiar with.

This guide walks you through the process of getting your company ready for mobile, from configuring your organization's settings to rolling out the Salesforce1 app and customizing it with your own branding. You'll learn how to quickly configure the items that appear in the navigation menu using the Salesforce1 Wizard. You'll also learn how to optimize page layouts, work with compact layouts, set up mobile notifications, and customize actions so your users can get important work done quickly from their mobile devices.

The Salesforce1 Admin Guide is an essential resource for Salesforce administrators who want to roll out enterprise mobile to their organizations. This guide introduces you to all of the declarative (point-and-click) tools needed to create a personalized mobile experience.

If, after reading this book, you want to venture into the world of developing for Salesforce1, take a look at the *Salesforce1 App Developer Guide*. Using a Developer Edition organization and a set of sample data and exercises, you can create custom actions, work with Visualforce pages, and learn about canvas apps and mobile UI design.

Introducing the Salesforce1 Apps

The Salesforce1 apps are Salesforce on the go! These enterprise-class mobile apps give your users real-time access to the same information that they see in the office, but organized for getting work done in those precioius free moments when they're between customer meetings, waiting for a flight...even when they're in line for coffee.

You can get Salesforce1 in different ways:

* As a downloadable app from the App Store and Google Play™.
* As a mobile browser app that runs in supported mobile browsers. This option doesn't require anything to be installed.

Supported Devices

The way users access Salesforce1 depends on whether they are using one of the downloadable apps or the mobile browser app.

Salesforce1 App	Supported Devices	Supported Mobile OS	Supported Mobile Browser
Downloadable app for iOS, v7.3 or later	iPhone 5 or later models iPad 4 or later models iPad mini 2 or later models Apple Watch (*push notifications only*)	iOS 8 or later	Not applicable
Downloadable app for Android, v7.3 or later	Android phones	Android 4.2 or later	Not applicable
Mobile browser app	iPhone 5 or later models iPad 4 or later models iPad mini 2 or later models	iOS 8 or later	Apple Safari Good Access
	Android phones Android tablets	Android 4.2 or later	Google Chrome Good Access
	Nokia Lumia 1020 and HTC 8X phones	Windows 8.1 Update	Microsoft Internet Explorer 11

Salesforce1 App	Supported Devices	Supported Mobile OS	Supported Mobile Browser
	Microsoft Surface 2 and Surface Pro 3 tablets		
	BlackBerry Z10 phones	BlackBerry OS 10.2 or later	BlackBerry Browser
	BlackBerry Z30 phones	BlackBerry OS 10.2.1.3175 or later	BlackBerry Browser

Getting Around in Salesforce1

Let's take a tour of the Salesforce1 mobile app.

When users log in to Salesforce1, the first thing they see is a landing page. The first item in the Salesforce1 navigation menu becomes a users' landing page by default. If your organization has Chatter enabled, and you haven't customized the Salesforce1 navigation menu to change the first item in the menu to something else, the user's Feed will be their landing page.

The Feed

The Chatter feed shows users their updates, updates to records and people they follow, and updates in groups they follow. Tapping a feed item displays all of the item's details. Pulling down on the feed reveals the search bar (1), sort and filter options (2), the feeds drop-down menu (3), and feed items (4).

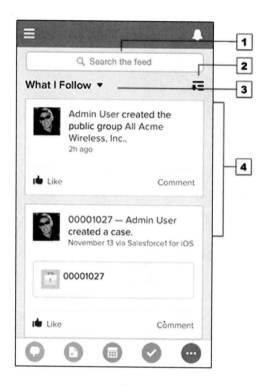

From the feed, record pages, and from elsewhere in Salesforce1, users access actions from the action bar.

The Action Bar and Menu

Depending on which feed or record page users are viewing, they see different actions in the action bar and action menu. From the feed, for example, they see a set of global actions. From a record page, however, they see a mix of productivity actions, standard and custom buttons, standard Chatter actions such as Post and File, and global and object-specific actions that are assigned to the layout for that record type. Users can tap ••• from the action bar to open the action menu, which contains the full set of actions that are available for the object.

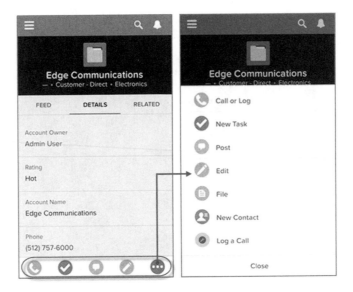

Note: You can find out more about the action bar in the appendix How Predefined Actions Are Ordered in the Salesforce1 Action Bar and List Item Actions or in the Salesforce Help.

Salesforce1 Navigation Menu

Anywhere users see ☰ in Salesforce1, they can tap it to access the navigation menu.

What your users see in the menu is determined by how you, as the administrator, have configured it, what's available in your organization, and what users have access to, based on their user permissions and profile.

1. Search box
2. Menu items—any items you place above the Smart Search Items element when you customize the navigation menu
3. Smart Search Items—includes a set of recently-searched objects in the Recent section and a larger set of supported objects under the More link
4. Apps section—contains any items you place below the Smart Search Items element

From the navigation menu, users can access the feed, objects, apps, tasks, notes, and any other item you've added to the menu.

The Record View

The record view is made up of the record feed, detail, and related information pages, which your users can swipe left and right to see. If your organization doesn't have Chatter enabled, the record view only includes the detail and related information pages.

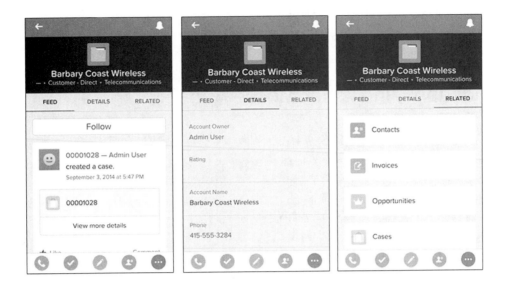

At the top of each record page is the record highlights area. The icon for standard objects is predefined in Salesforce, and you can select the icon for a custom object using the custom object's tab style.

You can customize the fields displayed in the record highlights by using compact layouts.

1. Back arrow—returns the user to the previous page
2. Record highlights—displays the first four fields that are assigned to the compact layout for the object

What else do I need to know?

From the top of most pages, users can access their notifications by tapping 🔔.

Users can create a new record by tapping **New** at the top of recent object pages, search pages, and related list pages. They can also create and update records by using actions, if create actions have been set up in the organization.

What about the Other Mobile Apps?

Wondering how the Salesforce1 app relates to the other Salesforce mobile products?

- SalesforceA gives administrators mobile access to essential organization management tasks. Use it to edit, unlock, freeze, and deactivate user accounts, reset passwords, and assign permission sets.

- The Salesforce mobile offerings still include Salesforce Classic Mobile. Salesforce Classic Mobile users might find that Salesforce1 is a better fit for their needs, but Salesforce Classic Mobile remains the best option if you need to create and edit in offline mode.

For more detailed information about the full suite of Salesforce mobile apps, see "Salesforce Mobile Products Overview" in the Salesforce Help.

CHAPTER 2   Get Your Organization Ready for Mobile: The Big Picture

Salesforce1 works for your users out of the box. If you do nothing to your organization, your users can still access its information and work in Salesforce1. However, as an administrator, you can significantly improve your mobile users' experience with Salesforce1 by taking the time to configure a few organization settings and customize how the data in your organization is displayed in a mobile environment.

In this book, we'll discuss how and where to do all of these.

- Define the users who can access Salesforce1.

- Help keep Salesforce1 users aware of important Salesforce activities by enabling in-app and push notifications.

- Allow the Salesforce1 downloadable apps to automatically cache frequently accessed Salesforce data to secure, persistent storage, so users can view data when their devices are offline. (This option is turned on by default.)

- Customize the options that are available in the Salesforce1 navigation menu, and the order in which items appear.

- Customize how data appears in Salesforce1.

- Make it easy and efficient to work in the field by creating actions that are tailored to your specific business activities and use cases.

- Customize Salesforce1 to match the look and feel of your company's branding.

All Salesforce1 customization options are available from the Setup menu, which you access from the upper-right corner of any Salesforce page. For your convenience, you can access many Salesforce1 settings pages more quickly from the Salesforce1 Quick Start page. In Salesforce Classic, from Setup, click **Salesforce1 Setup**. In Lightning Experience, from Setup, enter `Salesforce1 Quick Start` in the `Quick Find` box, then select **Salesforce1 Quick Start**.

CHAPTER 3
Configure Your Organization for Salesforce1

Make it easier for your mobile users to get work done in Salesforce1 by configuring a few settings in your organization. It doesn't take long, and your users will thank you for it!

With a few clicks, you can define which of your users can use Salesforce1, enable or disable key Salesforce1 features for your organization—such as in-app and push notifications, and offline access—and customize the Salesforce1 navigation menu. In this chapter, we'll go over all of these.

Unlock Salesforce1 with the Salesforce1 Wizard

The Salesforce1 Wizard provides an easy way to complete the essential setup tasks for Salesforce1.

The Salesforce1 Wizard is the ideal tool to quickly get your users started in Salesforce1. It provides a visual tour of Salesforce1's key point-and-click settings, which enables you to configure these options that apply to all users in your organization.

- Specify which items appear in the navigation menu
- Organize global actions
- Create a custom compact layout for contacts

The Salesforce1 Wizard gets you started with the basic setup tasks for Salesforce1, but there is a lot more customization you can do to further enhance your users' Salesforce1 experience.

If you're new to Salesforce1, or if you haven't done much customization or configuration for Salesforce1 in your organization, we recommend that you step through the wizard.

- In Salesforce Classic, you can get started in Setup by clicking **Salesforce1 Setup** and then **Launch Quick Start Wizard**.
- In Lightning Experience, from Setup, enter `Salesforce1` in the `Quick Find` box, select **Salesforce1 Quick Start**, and then click **Launch Quick Start Wizard**.

 Note: We recommend using Google Chrome for the Salesforce1 Wizard and the Salesforce1 Setup page. Microsoft Internet Explorer 9 or later and Mozilla Firefox are also supported.

After you've finished the wizard, you'll be directed to the Salesforce1 Setup page, which provides quick access to Setup pages and documentation for Salesforce1. For settings that are configured on a single page, the Salesforce1 Setup page includes direct links to those pages. In cases where the settings are available on multiple pages in Setup, we've provided links to relevant documentation about the setting.

Define Which Users Can Use Salesforce1

Regardless of whether your users prefer to use the Salesforce1 downloadable apps or the mobile browser app, with a few clicks you can control who has access and configure security settings.

Downloadable Apps

The Salesforce1 downloadable apps are connected apps. As a result, you can control the users who have access to the apps, as well as other security policies. By default, all users in your organization can log in to the Salesforce1 downloadable apps.

You can control security and access policies for each of the Salesforce1 downloadable apps, using settings components that are installed from the managed Salesforce1 connected apps package. These components need to be installed in Salesforce:

- Salesforce1 for Android
- Salesforce1 for iOS

These components are automatically installed when one of your users installs a Salesforce1 downloadable app from the App Store or Google Play on a mobile device and authenticates with your organization by logging in to the mobile app.

Alternatively, you can manually install the Salesforce1 and Chatter Apps connected apps package so you can review and modify the default security and access settings before rolling out the Salesforce1 downloadable apps to your users.

When the Salesforce1 connected apps components are installed, they're added to the Connected Apps page. (From Setup, enter `Connected Apps` in the `Quick Find` box, then select the option for managing connected apps.) Here, you can view and edit the settings for each of the apps, including controlling user access with profiles, permissions, and IP range restrictions. An error message is displayed if a restricted user attempts to log in to a Salesforce1 downloadable app.

Mobile Browser App

You can control whether users can access the Salesforce1 mobile browser app when they log in to Salesforce from a mobile browser. By default, the mobile browser app is turned on for your organization.

1. From Setup, enter `Salesforce1 Settings` in the `Quick Find` box, then select **Salesforce1 Settings**.
2. Select `Enable the Salesforce1 browser app` to allow all users in your organization to access the app. Deselect this option to turn off access to the app.
3. Click **Save**.

When this option is turned on, users who log in to Salesforce from a supported mobile browser are automatically directed to the Salesforce1 interface. Logging in from an unsupported mobile browser loads the full Salesforce site.

> ⊙ **Important:** Use of the full Salesforce site in a mobile browser isn't supported. While you can disable the mobile browser app for your organization—and individual users can turn off the app for themselves—regular use of the full site in a mobile browser isn't recommended. Your users may experience problems that Salesforce Customer Support won't investigate.

Enable or Disable Notifications

Notifications let your users know when certain events occur in Salesforce. For example, notifications let users know when they receive approval requests or when someone mentions them in Chatter.

You can enable or disable notifications on the Salesforce1 Notifications page in Setup. Notifications are enabled by default.

Two types of notifications can appear to Salesforce1 users.

In-app notifications

In-app notifications keep users aware of relevant activity while they're using Salesforce1. By tapping , a user can view the 20 most recent notifications received within the last 90 days.

If Salesforce Communities is enabled for your organization, users see notifications from all of the communities they're members of. To help users easily identify which community a notification came from, the community name is listed after the time stamp.

> Note: Enabling in-app notifications is an all-or-nothing process. Either they're on for everyone, or off for everyone. Mobile users can't customize, enable, or disable in-app notifications for themselves.

Push notifications

Push notifications are alerts that appear on a mobile device when a user has installed the Salesforce1 downloadable app but isn't using it. These alerts can consist of text, icons, and sounds, depending on the device type. If an administrator enables push notifications for your organization, users can choose individually whether to receive push notifications on their devices.

Some notifications include text that your users enter in Salesforce. To ensure that sensitive information isn't distributed through a third-party service without proper authorization, push notifications include minimal content (such as a user's name) unless you enable full content in push notifications. For example, suppose an in-app notification reads: "Allison Wheeler mentioned you: @John Smith, heads-up! New sales strategy for Acme account." By default, the equivalent push notification would be "Allison Wheeler mentioned you." However, if you enabled full content in push notifications, this push notification would include the same (full) content as the in-app notification.

By enabling the option to include full content in push notifications, you're agreeing on behalf of your company to the terms and conditions displayed when you save the setting. For details, see "Salesforce1 Mobile App Notifications" in the Salesforce Help.

Approval Request Notifications in Salesforce1

Users can receive approval requests as notifications in Salesforce1 and can access them by tapping or from the Approval Requests item in the navigation menu.

However, some caveats apply to how approval notifications work in Salesforce1.

- If you enable notifications in Salesforce1, keep in mind that approvers may view this list of fields on a mobile device. Select only the fields necessary for users to decide whether to approve or reject records.

- Salesforce1 notifications for approval requests aren't sent to queues. For each approval step involving a queue, we recommend adding individual users as assigned approvers, so at least those individuals can receive the approval request notifications in Salesforce1. To have both queues and individual users as assigned approvers, select `Automatically assign to approver(s)` instead of `Automatically assign to queue` in the approval step.

- Unlike notifications for approval requests in email, notifications for approval requests in Salesforce1 are sent only to users who have access to the record being approved. Assigned approvers who don't have record access can still receive email approval notifications, but they can't complete the approval request until someone grants them record access.

- Individual users can opt in or out of approval request notifications in both email and Salesforce1 via the `Receive Approval Request Emails` user field.

Salesforce1 Mobile App Offline Access

Salesforce1 can cache recently accessed data so it's available when a user's device is offline or unable to connect to Salesforce. Offline access is currently read-only, and is available in the Salesforce1 downloadable apps for iOS and Android devices.

Offline access is enabled the first time a user in your organization installs one of the Salesforce1 downloadable apps. You can manage this setting on the Salesforce1 Offline page in Setup.

EDITIONS

Available in: Salesforce Classic

Available in: **All** editions except **Database.com**

With offline access turned on, the app automatically caches a user's most recently accessed records for the objects listed in the Recent section of the Salesforce1 navigation menu, and a user's recent dashboards. Recently accessed records are determined by a user's activities in both the mobile app and the full Salesforce site. In addition, the app caches much of the data that a user accesses during a Salesforce1 session.

Cached data is encrypted and stored in a secure, persistent data store.

This table lists the data and Salesforce1 elements that are available offline.

Salesforce1 Element	Available for Offline Use
Navigation Menu	Yes
Global Search	Previous searches only

Salesforce1 Element	Available for Offline Use
Notifications	Previously viewed only
Feeds, Groups, and People	Previously viewed only
Salesforce Today	Main page and mobile event records if previously view
Salesforce Events	Previously viewed only
Recent Objects	Yes (top five)
Other Objects	No
Record Details	Yes (30 most recent records)
Related Records	Previously viewed only
List Views	Previously viewed only
Tasks	Only tasks from the first page of the My Tasks list (up to 10 tasks), and only if the list was previously viewed or after the user manually updates the cache
Dashboards	Yes (top five)
Approvals (submit, approve, or reject)	No
Visualforce pages	No
Canvas Apps	No
Lightning Pages	No
Settings	Yes

Cached data is refreshed when a user switches to Salesforce1. If a user switches to another app, the user's cached data is automatically refreshed if the existing data store is over one hour old.

Users can manually cache their data at any time—for example, before switching into airplane mode or entering an area with no service. From the Salesforce1 navigation menu, select **Settings** > **Offline Cache** > **Cache Now**.

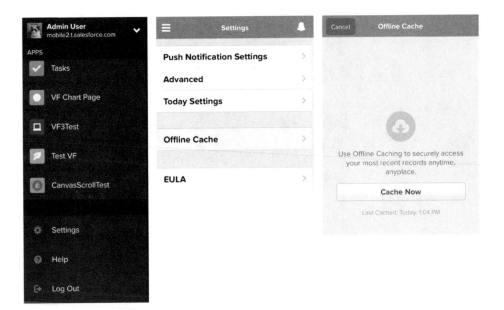

 Note: The cache is saved for two weeks. Users can clear the cache by logging out of the Salesforce1 app.

Customize the Salesforce1 Navigation Menu

Before you can send your users out on their mobile adventure in Salesforce1, they need a map to point the way to their destination. The Salesforce1 navigation menu is that map. And it's up to you to draw it for them. Help your mobile users get work done faster and more easily by configuring which items appear in the navigation menu and in which order.

The ▤ icon in the Salesforce1 header opens the navigation menu.

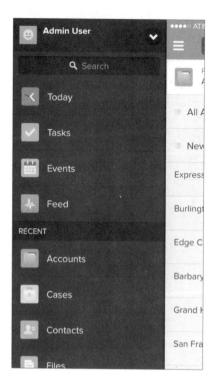

As an administrator, you can customize what the menu contains in Setup by entering *Navigation menu* in the *Quick Find* box, then selecting **Navigation menu**.

What You Can Include

Depending on how your organization is configured and what your users have access to, they might see some or all of these items in their navigation menu.

Menu Item	Description
Approval Requests	Displays a list of the user's pending approvals. Users can tap an approval item and approve or reject it from within Salesforce1. Available in the Salesforce1 downloadable app for iOS and the Salesforce1 mobile browser app.
Canvas apps	Appears for organizations that have enabled a canvas app to appear in the Salesforce1 navigation menu.

Menu Item	Description
Dashboards	Availability depends on edition and user permissions. If you don't include this item in the menu, a Dashboards item is automatically added to the set of Smart Search Items.
Events	Lists events that are owned by the user, that the user created for him- or herself, and that the user or a user's groups are invited to.
Feed	Appears for organizations that have Chatter enabled.
Lightning component tabs (Beta)	Only custom Lightning components that have a Lightning component tab associated with them can appear in the Salesforce1 navigation menu.
Lightning Pages	Custom Salesforce1 app pages.
Groups	Appears for organizations that have Chatter enabled. If you don't include this item in the menu, a Groups item is automatically added to the set of Smart Search Items.
Paused Flow Interviews	Displays a list of flow interviews that the user paused. An interview is a running instance of a flow. Users can tap an interview and resume or delete it from within Salesforce1. Available in the Salesforce1 mobile browser app only.
People	Appears for organizations that have Chatter enabled. If you don't include this item in the menu, a People item is automatically added to the set of Smart Search Items.
Smart Search Items	Adds Salesforce objects to the Recent section in the menu. This item also adds a set of recently-searched objects to the Recent section and adds the More item so users can access all the objects they have permission to use and that are supported in Salesforce1. If you don't include this item in the navigation menu, users can't access any objects in Salesforce1. Note: If your users don't yet have a history of recent objects, they initially see a set of default objects in the Recent section. It can take up to 15 days for the objects that users work with regularly in both Salesforce1 and the full Salesforce site to appear in the Recent section. To make objects appear under Recent sooner, users can pin them from the search results screen in the full site.
Tasks	Lists of a user's open and closed tasks and tasks that have been delegated.

Menu Item	Description
Today	An app that helps users plan for and manage their day by integrating mobile calendar events with associated Salesforce tasks, accounts, and contacts. The app also allows users to instantly join conference calls, quickly log notes about events, and more. Available in the Salesforce1 downloadable apps only.
Visualforce page tabs	Only Visualforce pages with the `Available for Salesforce mobile apps` checkbox selected will display in Salesforce1.

We'll touch briefly on Visualforce pages in a later chapter. To delve even deeper, see "Extending Salesforce1 with Visualforce Pages" in the *Salesforce1 App Developer Guide*.

How the Salesforce1 Navigation Menu Works

- The first item in the Selected list becomes your users' Salesforce1 landing page.
- You can't set different menu configurations for different types of users.
- When organizing the menu items, put the items that users will use most at the top. The Smart Search Items element can expand into a set of eight or more menu items and it might end up pushing other elements below the scroll point if you put it near the top of the menu. Anything you put below the Smart Search Items element appears in the Apps section of the navigation menu.
- Before you can include Visualforce pages, Lightning Pages, or Lightning components in the Salesforce1 navigation menu, create tabs for them. From Setup, enter `Tabs` in the `Quick Find` box, then select **Tabs**.
- Anything that is represented by a tab in Salesforce—such as standard and custom objects, Visualforce pages, the Feed, People, or Groups—is visible for a user in the Salesforce1 menu, based on the user's profile settings. For example, if a user is assigned to a profile that has the Groups tab set to Tab Hidden, the user won't see the Groups menu item in Salesforce1, even though an administrator has included it in the menu.

Some objects are excluded from the Recent section in the Salesforce1 navigation menu, even if you accessed them recently.

- Tasks and events
- People, groups, and dashboards, if these items were added directly to the navigation menu
- List views, which are shown only on object home pages, not in the navigation menu
- Objects that aren't available in Salesforce1, including any objects that don't have a tab in the full Salesforce site

About the Dashboards, People, and Groups Menu Items

If you don't add the Dashboards, People, or Groups menu items to the Selected list for the navigation menu, then they're automatically included in the Smart Search Items set of objects and show up in the Recent section of the menu in Salesforce1. If you do add Dashboards, People, or Groups individually to the Selected list for the navigation menu, then they show up outside of the Recent section and their location in the Salesforce1 menu can be customized, just like Tasks, Today, and other individual menu items.

Pin an Object into the Recent Section

Users can customize the objects that appear in the Recent section of the Salesforce1 navigation menu. If they search for an object in the full site, they can hover their mouse over the object name and click 📌 to pin it to the top of the search results. The order of pinned objects in the full site determines the order of the objects that stick to the top of the Recent section of the navigation menu. However, pinning objects in this way causes the unpinned objects remaining in the Recent section to drop into the **More** element.

CHAPTER 4 Customize How Your Data Appears in Salesforce1

In this chapter ...

- How Page Layouts Work in Salesforce1
- Working with Compact Layouts

After configuring your organization settings for the Salesforce1 app, consider what else you can optimize in the full Salesforce site to give your users the best possible mobile experience.

Two factors in Salesforce affect how information is displayed in Salesforce1. One has been around for a while: page layouts. The other is newer: compact layouts. You'll learn about both in this chapter.

How Page Layouts Work in Salesforce1

Use the enhanced page layout editor to customize the layout of an object's record detail pages, configure actions, and adjust which fields and related lists appear in Salesforce1.

In Salesforce1, page layouts drive these areas of the mobile experience.

EDITIONS

Available in: Salesforce Classic

Available in all editions

Record Related Information and Detail Pages

When you view a record in Salesforce1, you see the fields, Visualforce pages, and related lists that are based on the record type and the user's profile. Related lists show up as single-line cards containing the name of the page or related list. Tapping the related list card displays its details.

Mobile Cards

You can add expanded lookups, components, canvas apps, and Visualforce pages to the Mobile Cards section of your page layout to have them show up as mobile cards in Salesforce1. The elements you place in this section don't show up on a record's detail page in the full Salesforce site. They appear only on the record's related information page in Salesforce1.

 Note: In organizations that are created after Spring '14, the Twitter component is added by default to the Mobile Cards section of page layouts for objects that support it.

Actions

In Salesforce1, actions in the Salesforce1 and Lightning Experience Actions section of a page layout appear in the action bar and action menu on the object's record pages.

Here are the record detail page, related information page, and action menu for a sample account, Edge Communications:

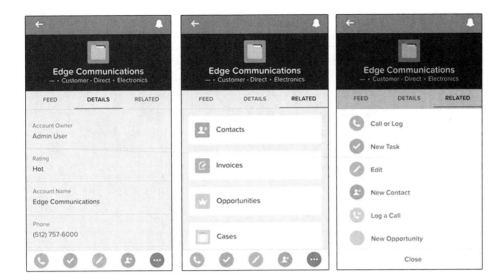

Rethink Your Page Layouts for Mobile

Page layouts containing dozens of fields and lots of related lists might be manageable when viewing records on a computer screen, but on a small mobile device, viewing that same record can be overwhelming. People accessing information using a mobile device are looking for a quick way to get what they need, and making your users sift through hundreds of fields and related lists just doesn't make sense.

For example, let's say you have a custom account page layout for Express Logistics and Transport, which has 32 standard and custom fields. That may not seem like a lot of fields, but in a mobile context, fields add up quickly. In the full Salesforce site, the account detail page for Express Logistics and Transport would look like this:

In Salesforce1, the same account detail page looks like this:

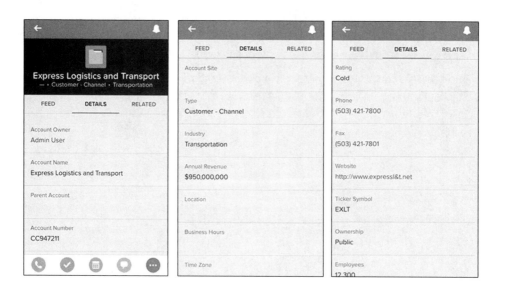

Three pages of scrolling, and that's from a page layout with only 32 fields! If you were a mobile user trying to find specific fields in a record detail with dozens of fields on your phone, you'd have to scroll... and scroll... and scroll. It's not the best user experience and it's definitely not good for your users' productivity.

You have two options for handling page layouts for your mobile users: re-engineer your existing page layouts, or create new page layouts that are mobile-friendly from the outset.

Tips for Optimizing Page Layouts for Mobile

In many cases, creating a new mobile-only page layout may not make sense. Here are some tips and tricks to making your existing page layouts more mobile friendly.

When optimizing a page layout, consider:

- What are the important things to see at a glance?
- What are the important moments for your users when they're working in Salesforce1?
- What actions or processes can you automate so that your users don't have to manually do them?

The Key: Organize and Minimize Fields

- Use sections to organize information logically, putting the most important things at the top of the page so they show up first. Your users don't want to search for fields individually. Organizing similar fields in sections will help your users find what they need. They can then easily scroll down the page to the section they care about.
- For accounts, contacts, and leads, you don't need to put phone or email fields near the top. They're already quickly accessible via the 📞 and ✉ icons on each record page's action bar.
- You don't need to keep fields in one column, as the page will render dynamically based on the device that's viewing it. A phone will reorder the fields into a single column, and a tablet or desktop will show two columns.
- Put the most important fields into the compact layout—which drives record highlights and record preview cards in Salesforce1—so they're available right up front, and so your mobile users don't have to drill into the record detail. We'll get into compact layouts in more detail soon.
- Keep the number of required fields to a minimum. Setting a field to required means it must appear on the detail page of all page layouts, so consider whether each field is truly required. You might have to convince stakeholders that a field isn't actually necessary for a record to be saved.
- If available in your organization, think about using record types so that fields that aren't common to all records don't have to appear on all records.
- To reduce the number of fields on a screen, consider using default values for new records instead of having the user enter the data.

Working with Compact Layouts

Page layouts aren't the only thing that you can use to customize how Salesforce data appears in a mobile environment. Compact layouts are used in Salesforce1 and Lightning Experience to display a record's key fields at a glance.

Creating and customizing compact layouts for objects isn't required for Salesforce1, because system defaults are provided out of the box. However, we recommend using compact layouts to put important fields into object record headers—and elsewhere—to help your mobile users get the information they need quickly.

In the full Salesforce site, compact layouts determine which fields appear in the Chatter feed item that appears after a user creates a record with a quick action.

In Salesforce1, the first four fields that you assign to a compact layout appear in:

* An object's record highlights area
* Expanded lookup cards on a record's related information page

For example, here are screenshots of a merchandise record page in Salesforce1 before and after customizing the compact layout for the object.

If you put the key fields that your mobile users need on the compact layout for an object, they can get that information quickly just by scanning the highlights area of the record page.

If you don't create custom compact layouts for an object, all the object's record highlight fields, preview cards, and action-related feed items are driven by a read-only, system default compact layout that contains a predefined set of fields. After you create one or more custom compact layouts, you can set one as the primary compact layout for the object. The primary compact layout is then used as the default for that object.

About Compact Layouts

Here are a few more more tidbits about how compact layouts work.

Compact layouts support all field types except:

- text area
- long text area
- rich text area
- multi-select picklist

Users who don't have access to certain fields in Salesforce won't see them on the compact layout.

Removing a field from a page layout doesn't remove it from the object's compact layout. The two layout types are independent.

Compact Layouts and Record Types

If you have record types associated with an object, you can override the primary compact layout assignment and assign specific compact layouts to different record types. If you don't set any record type overrides, all record types use the object's primary compact layout by default.

To find out more about compact layouts and record types, see "Assign Compact Layouts to Record Types" in the Salesforce Help.

CHAPTER 5   Using Actions in Salesforce1

In this chapter ...

- Working with Quick Actions
- Object-Specific versus Global Actions
- Action Layouts
- Using Predefined Values in Actions
- Custom Actions
- Actions and Page Layouts
- Action Guidelines and Best Practices

As an administrator, you can enable valuable micro-moments for all of your users by creating unique actions. When thinking about what actions you might want to create specifically for Salesforce1, ask your users what they wish they could do in the mobile context.

For example, an administrator at a food service company could create an "Emergency Order" action that allows their delivery drivers to immediately order extra or missing food items using their mobile phone while still at a customer site. Creating actions for Salesforce1 can drive adoption in your organization and make you a hero to your users!

In this chapter, we'll learn about types and categories of actions, how to create and customize them in Salesforce using point-and-click tools, and how they can help mobile users get essential work done while away from the office.

Working with Quick Actions

Actions enable users to do more in Salesforce and in Salesforce1. For example, create or update records and log calls directly in the Chatter feed or from users' mobile devices.

Create actions and add them to the Chatter publisher on the home page, on the Chatter tab, in Chatter groups, and on record detail pages. In Salesforce Classic, actions appear in the Chatter publisher. In Lightning Experience, actions appear in different areas of the user interface, depending on the action's type. In Salesforce1, actions appear in the action bar, its associated action menu, and as list-item actions.

Salesforce1 Actions in the Action Bar and Action Menu

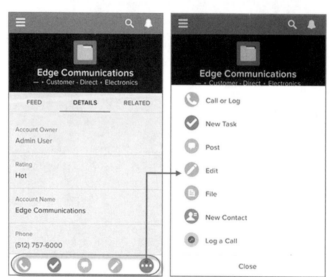

After creating quick actions, you can customize them. Quick actions have their own action layouts, which let you specify which fields are included in the action, and in which order.

Follow these steps when setting up actions for Salesforce1.

1. Create a global or object-specific action.

2. Customize the action's layout, choosing the fields users see when they use it.

3. If you created an object-specific action, add it to one or more of that object's page layouts. If you created a global action, add it to a global publisher layout.

4. Set predefined field values for required fields, where possible.

Let's learn a little more about the types and categories of actions. First we'll look at global and object-specific actions.

Object-Specific versus Global Actions

Regardless of what kind of action you're going to create, the first thing you need to determine is whether it should be object-specific or global. This decision should be based on whether you need your action to be explicitly tied to an object, and where you want the action to display.

Let's go over the differences.

Object-Specific Actions

You create object-specific actions in the context of the object. From Setup, click **Customize**, choose the object for which you want to create an action, and then click **Buttons, Links, and Actions**. You can add an object-specific action only to page layouts for that object.

There are five types of object-specific actions.

- Object-specific actions create records that are automatically associated with related records. For example, you add an object-specific action on the Account object that creates contacts. If a user creates a contact with that action on the detail page for the Acme account, that new contact is automatically associated with Acme.
- Object-specific update actions make it easy for users to edit records. You can define the fields that are available for update.
- Object-specific Log a Call actions let users enter notes about calls, meetings, or other interactions that are related to a specific record.
- Object-specific custom actions are Visualforce pages or canvas apps that let users interact with or create records that have a relationship to an object record. The Visualforce page for an object-specific custom action must include the standard controller for the relevant object. For example, use the standard contact controller to create a custom action that lets users import a contact's Twitter profile and add that information to a contact record.
- Send email actions, available only on cases, give users access to a simplified version of the Case Feed Email action on Salesforce1.

Global Actions

You create global actions in a different place in Setup than you create object-specific actions. To create a global action, from Setup, enter *Actions* in the Quick Find box, then select **Global Actions**. They're called *global actions* because they can be put anywhere actions are supported.

Global create actions enable users to create object records, but there's no automatic relationship between the record that's created and any other record.

Add Log a Call actions to global layouts to let users record call details from global pages, such as the Home page and the Chatter tab in the full Salesforce site, or the Feed or Groups pages in Salesforce1.

Use a Visualforce page or a canvas app to create a global custom action for tasks that don't require users to interact with or create records that have a relationship to a specific object. For more information, see Custom Actions on page 40.

 Note:

- Actions to create records for an object that is the detail object in a master-detail relationship must be object-specific, not global.
- Chatter groups with customers don't support global create, log a call, or custom actions and display only standard Chatter actions, such as Post, File, Link, and Poll.

After you create an object-specific or global action, you must add it to a page layout or the global publisher layout before it will appear in Salesforce1. For more information, see Actions and Page Layouts on page 41.

For a list of supported objects for object-specific and global actions, see "Object-Specific Actions" and "Global Actions" in the Salesforce Help.

Action Categories and Types

Actions that you create can be global or object-specific, but those aren't the only kinds of actions available in Salesforce and Salesforce1. Other types of actions, some predefined by Salesforce, are also available for you to put to work for your users.

There are several categories of actions, such as standard Chatter actions, nonstandard actions, default actions, mobile smart actions, custom actions, and productivity actions.

Category	Description	Included Actions	Where They Display
Standard Chatter actions	Standard Chatter actions are included when Chatter is enabled. You can customize the order in which these actions appear, but you can't edit their properties. Standard Chatter actions require that feed tracking for objects is enabled.	Post, File, Link, Poll, Question, Thanks (Work.com), and Announcements (Groups)	Salesforce and Salesforce1 Only Post and Announcements are supported in Lightning Experience

Category	Description	Included Actions	Where They Display
Nonstandard actions	Nonstandard actions are actions that you create and customize yourself. The actions can be global or object-specific.		Salesforce and Salesforce1
Default actions	Default actions are Salesforce predefined actions to get you and your users started using actions in your organization. Add default actions to publisher layouts to make them available to your users in the full Salesforce site and the action bar in Salesforce1. Default actions are supported on account, case, contact, lead, and opportunity objects.	Depends on the object. For a list of global actions and which default actions apply to which object, see "Default Actions" in the Salesforce Help.	Salesforce and Salesforce1
Mobile smart actions	Mobile smart actions are a set of preconfigured actions, just like default actions, and are supported on the same list of objects. Mobile smart actions appear as a single element in the page layout editor. In Salesforce1, the Mobile Smart Actions element expands to a set of distinct create actions that enable users to create records directly in the feed.	Depends on the object. For a list of which actions the Mobile Smart Actions element expands to include for each object, see "Mobile Smart Actions" in the Salesforce Help.	Salesforce1
Custom actions	*Custom actions* are Visualforce pages or canvas apps with functionality that you define. For example, you can create a custom action so that users can write comments that are longer than 5,000 characters, or create one that	Custom actions that you create.	Salesforce and Salesforce1 Not supported in Chatter groups with customers

Category	Description	Included Actions	Where They Display
	integrates a video-conferencing application so that support agents can communicate visually with customers. Custom actions can be global or object-specific.		
Productivity actions	Productivity actions are predefined by Salesforce and are attached to a limited set of objects. You can't edit or delete productivity actions. Productivity actions appear on these objects. • Account • Contact • Event • Lead • User • User Profile	Depends on the object. The actions include Send Email, Log a Call, Map, View Website, and Read News.	Salesforce (Lightning Experience only) and Salesforce1

Which actions are available in the full Salesforce site depends on whether your organization has Chatter, feed tracking, and actions in the publisher enabled. Actions in Salesforce1 don't rely on whether Chatter or actions in the publisher are enabled. For how Chatter enablement affects action visibility, see Actions with and without Chatter on page 62.

Within the categories of actions, you can have different types of actions, depending on their function.

• *Create actions* let users create records. They're different from the Quick Create and Create New features on the Salesforce home page, because create actions respect validation rules and field requiredness, and you can choose each action's fields.

• *Log a call actions* let users record the details of phone calls or other customer interactions. These call logs are saved as completed tasks.

• *Question actions* enable users to ask and search for questions about the records that they're working with.

- *Send email actions*, available only on cases, give users access to a simplified version of the Case Feed Email action on Salesforce1.
- *Update actions* let users make changes to a record.

For create, log-a-call, and custom actions, you can create either object-specific actions or global actions. Update actions must be object-specific.

Action Layouts

Just as object record pages have page layouts that can be customized, actions have action layouts that can be customized. You can add, remove, or reorder fields on the action layout to present only the essential items your users need when they're taking the action.

To customize the layouts of your global actions, in Setup, enter `Actions` in the `Quick Find` box, then select **Global Actions**. (If you're in Salesforce Classic, click **Publisher Layouts**.) Then click **Layout** next to a global action in the list.

To customize the layouts of your object-specific actions, from the management settings for an object, find Buttons, Links, and Actions.

- If you're using Salesforce Classic, from Setup, enter an object name in the `Quick Find` box, select **Buttons, Links, and Actions**, and then click **Layout** next to an action in the list.
- If you're using Lightning Experience, from Setup, enter `Object Manager` in the `Quick Find` box, select **Object Manager**, and then scroll down to the Buttons, Links, and Actions section. Then click **Edit** next to the name of an action.

The first time you view the layout for an action you've created, certain fields are prepopulated: target object default fields, standard required fields, and any custom universally required fields.

Use the action layout editor to specify which fields to include in the layout.

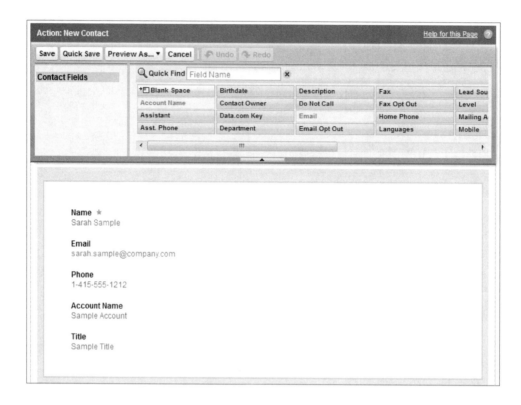

The upper part of the editor contains a palette, and below the palette is the action layout. The palette contains fields from the action's target object that you can add to the action layout, except for the following unsupported field types:

- Record type fields
- Read-only field types such as roll-up summary, formula, and auto-number fields
- Read-only system fields such as `Created By` or `Last Modified By`

Inactive Fields

Fields that are already on the action layout still appear on the palette but are inactive. When you select an inactive field on the palette, Salesforce highlights the field on the action layout.

Field Type Conversion

If you convert a field's type from one that is supported for actions to a type that isn't supported, Salesforce removes the field from the action layout. If you convert the field back to a supported type without changing the action layout, Salesforce automatically adds the field back to the layout. If you edit the layout and then convert the field back to a supported type, add the field back to the layout manually.

Layouts Used for Log a Call Actions

A Log a Call action takes the active task page layout except under the following conditions:

- Suppose that your organization has a custom Log a Call action for an object. The custom action takes the custom action layout defined for it.

- Now suppose that your organization has a custom Log a Call global action. That action takes the custom layout defined for it, unless you also have a custom Log a Call action for an object. (A custom action on an object overrides a custom global action.)

To display the simpler New Task form to Salesforce1 users, enable the form in Activity Settings and ensure that the layout used includes a subject field.

Layout Auditing

Salesforce tracks action layout customization in the setup audit trail history.

Using Predefined Values in Actions

Setting up *predefined values* for certain fields on actions can increase your mobile users' productivity and optimize the action for the mobile environment at the same time.

When you configure action layouts, it's better to use fewer fields. Most users, especially mobile users, don't like to fill in a lot of required fields. They want to get things done and move on to their next task. A good way to use fewer fields in action layouts is to set predefined values for as many fields as possible. The more fields you can set predefined values for, the more you can remove from the layout and make the action easier and quicker to use. Balance ease of use with the need for required information. However, don't remove required fields from an action layout without setting a predefined value for those fields, or when a user applies that action, the record won't save properly.

If you set predefined values for fields on object records created through an action, you don't need to add those fields to the action layout. For example, when you configure an action that lets users create opportunities, set Prospecting as the predefined value for the `Stage` field. All new opportunities users create through that action are automatically assigned to the prospecting stage. You can remove the `Stage` field from the action's layout, because the field is going to be assigned a value automatically.

To set predefined values for object-specific actions, from your object management settings, select an object, and then scroll down to the Buttons, Links, and Actions section. To set predefined values for global actions, enter `Actions` in the `Quick Find` box, then select **Global Actions**. On the action list page for either type, click the name of the action, and then click **New** in the Predefined Field Values related list.

You can set predefined values for any field available in the action layout editor, with these exceptions.

- Rich text area fields
- Multi-select picklists

- Read-only field types like auto-number, formula, and roll-up summary fields

Predefined values for fields on actions are different from default values that you can set for fields on records. If a field is included in an action, it can have both a predefined value set for the action *and* a default value set. If a field on an action has both a predefined value and a default value set, the action uses the predefined value, not the default value.

On object-specific actions, the predefined value can include references to the source object and its related objects.

 Tip: You can remove a required field from the action layout, but make sure that the field has a predefined value. Otherwise, users can't create records.

Custom Actions

Custom actions are Visualforce pages or canvas apps with functionality that you define. For example, you can create a custom action so that users can write comments that are longer than 5,000 characters, or create one that integrates a video-conferencing application so that support agents can communicate visually with customers.

You can create object-specific and global custom actions.

Object-specific custom actions are Visualforce pages or canvas apps that let users interact with or create records that have a relationship to an object record. The Visualforce page for an object-specific custom action must include the standard controller for the relevant object. For example, use the standard contact controller to create a custom action that lets users import a contact's Twitter profile and add that information to a contact record.

Use a Visualforce page or a canvas app to create a global custom action for tasks that don't require users to interact with or create records that have a relationship to a specific object. Canvas apps that you want to use as custom actions require Publisher as a location. Visualforce pages that you want to use as global custom actions can't use standard controllers. For example, if you want a custom action that lets users enter a street address and see a map, the local time, and the local weather. For this action, create a Visualforce page that doesn't use any of the standard controllers, and add it as a custom global action.

You create a Visualforce custom action in the same way you create a regular object-specific or global action. However, when you select the action type, select Custom Visualforce instead of Create a Record or Log a Call. Then, select the Visualforce page you want to use for the action.

Creating custom actions for canvas apps is more complex, and we won't discuss them in depth here. You can find out more about canvas apps and custom actions in the *Salesforce1 App Developer Guide*.

 Note: Chatter groups with customers don't support global create, log a call, or custom actions and display only standard Chatter actions, such as Post, File, Link, and Poll.

Actions and Page Layouts

Before an action can appear in both the full Salesforce site and Salesforce1, you must add it to a page layout.

Global Page Layouts

What is a global page? The Home page, the User Profile page, and the Chatter home pages are all examples of global pages in the full Salesforce site. A *global publisher layout* drives the actions displayed on these pages. A global publisher layout is like a page layout, but it contains only the Quick Actions in the Salesforce Classic Publisher and Salesforce1 and Lightning Experience Actions sections.

Use global publisher layouts to customize actions that appear on Chatter publishers for global pages such as the Home page and the Chatter page. Global publisher layouts also drive the actions that users see in the action bar and action menu on the Feed and People pages in Salesforce1. Global publisher layouts can be composed only from global actions.

After creating global publisher layouts, you can assign them to different user profiles to customize which actions users see by default on global pages.

To create a custom global publisher layout, or to customize the default global layout, in Setup, enter `Publisher Layouts` in the `Quick Find` box, then select **Publisher Layouts**. After you've defined a global publisher layout, click **Publisher Layout Assignment** to assign it to user profiles.

Object Page Layouts

Object-specific actions can be added only to page layouts for the object to which they are assigned. However, you can add global actions to the page layout of any object that supports actions.

You can customize the actions that show up on object page layouts—like those for Account, Opportunity, and Contact—by using the page layout editor. Actions added to the Quick Actions in the Salesforce Classic Publisher section of an object's page layout appear in the Chatter publisher for that object in the full Salesforce site. Actions added to the Salesforce1 and Lightning Experience Actions section of an object's page layout appear in the action bar on the object's record pages in Salesforce1.

If you haven't customized the Quick Actions in the Salesforce Classic Publisher section of a page layout, the actions that appear in the publisher for that object default to the actions that are assigned to the global publisher layout. Upon overriding, the actions default to the standard actions—Post, File, Link, Poll, Question, and Thanks—regardless of what actions were assigned to the global publisher layout.

If you haven't customized the Salesforce1 and Lightning Experience Actions section of a page layout, the actions for that object default to a set of predefined actions. If you have customized actions in the Quick

Actions in the Salesforce Classic Publisher section, and have saved the layout, the Salesforce1 and Lightning Experience Actions section inherits the actions from the Quick Actions in the Salesforce Classic Publisher section when you click to override.

Action Guidelines and Best Practices

Actions are a great way to let your users get work done quickly. As an administrator, you're in a prime position to give them the exact actions that they need.

When considering what kinds of actions to create, or even when creating the actions themselves, keep these suggestions in mind.

- When customizing action layouts, consider what your users will do with them. Minimalism is key. Include only the fields that are necessary for them and for whomever handles the cases, calls, or records that result from those actions.

- Don't use actions for simple navigation shortcuts. They're designed to perform a function.

- Give your actions task-oriented names that tell your users what they do. Use terms such as New, Create, Share, Update, or Import. Keep names short and descriptive.

- Create a global action if you're contemplating something that your users need to do that isn't tied to a specific object and that you want to be accessible from anywhere.

- Use the `Description` field to create notes for yourself about each action. Notes are especially useful if you're creating several similar actions for different record types, for example. The description appears in the list of buttons, links, and actions for object-specific actions, or in the list of global actions, as well as on the detail page for the action. Your notes aren't visible to users.

- There is no hard limit to the number of fields you can add to an action layout. However, for optimum usability, we recommend a maximum of 8 fields. Adding more than 20 fields can severely impact user efficiency. To reduce the number of fields in your layout, you can create predefined values for the required fields, and then remove those fields from your layout. You can set predefined field values from the action detail page.

CHAPTER 6 Visualforce Pages and Salesforce1

In this chapter ...

- Get Your Visualforce Pages into Salesforce1
- Visualforce Page Support in Salesforce1

You can use Visualforce to extend the Salesforce1 app and give your mobile users the functionality that they need while on the go.

For example, you can include a Visualforce page that shows a mobile user the location of a selected account on a Google map. In Salesforce1, this page appears as a mobile card on the account record's related information page.

Get Your Visualforce Pages into Salesforce1

Visualforce pages must be enabled for mobile use before they can display in Salesforce1. You can do this in Setup by entering `Visualforce Pages` in the `Quick Find` box, then selecting **Visualforce Pages**, then click **Edit** next to a page name, and select the `Available for Salesforce mobile apps` checkbox on that page.

> 💡 Tip: Just because you've enabled a Visualforce page for mobile doesn't mean that it's automatically mobile friendly. Before exposing existing Visualforce pages in Salesforce1, consider how they'll look and function on mobile phones and tablets. Most likely, you'll want to create a new page specifically for mobile form factors.

Visualforce pages can display in these areas of the Salesforce1 user interface:

- The navigation menu, via a Visualforce tab
- The action bar, via a custom action
- Mobile cards on a record's related information page
- Overridden standard buttons, or custom buttons and links
- Embedded in record detail page layouts
- Lightning pages

If you want to dig deeper into customizing Salesforce1 with Visualforce, and discover lots of best practices to use when designing your pages for Salesforce1, check out the Visualforce chapters of the *Salesforce1 App Developer Guide*.

Visualforce Page Support in Salesforce1

Keep these considerations in mind when you're working with Visualforce pages in Salesforce1.

- Standard tabs, custom object tabs, and list views that are overridden with a Visualforce page aren't supported in Salesforce1. The Visualforce page is shown for full site users, but Salesforce1 users will see the default Salesforce1 page for the object. This restriction exists to maintain the Salesforce1 experience for objects.
- You can also enable Visualforce pages for Salesforce1 through the metadata API by editing the `isAvailableInTouch` field on the ApexPage object.
- The `Salesforce Classic Mobile Ready` checkbox on Visualforce Tab setup pages is for Salesforce Classic Mobile only and has no effect on Visualforce pages in the Salesforce1 apps.

CHAPTER 7 Make the Salesforce1 App Yours with Custom Branding

In this chapter ...

- How Salesforce1 Branding Works
- Tips for Branding Your Salesforce1 App

You can customize the Salesforce1 mobile app to match the look and feel of your company's branding, so the app is instantly recognizable to your mobile users. Custom branding is displayed in all of the Salesforce1 apps.

How Salesforce1 Branding Works

You can customize branding for your Salesforce1 app. From Setup, enter `Salesforce1 Branding` in the `Quick Find` box, then select **Salesforce1 Branding**.

Prerequisites

Images that you upload to customize the Salesforce1 app are stored in a Documents folder named Salesforce1 Branding Resources. For this reason, the Documents object must be enabled for your organization before administrators can view and modify the Salesforce1 Branding page. (The Documents tab doesn't need to be visible, however.)

For users of the Salesforce1 mobile browser app to see custom branding, Documents must be enabled for your organization. For the Salesforce1 downloadable apps, users must also have "Read" user permissions on Documents.

What You Can Customize

Element	Description
Brand Color	The color for key user interface elements such as the header, buttons, and search bar.
	Based on the brand color you select, contrasting colors for user interface elements such as borders for the navigation menu, the notifications list, and button text are automatically defined.
	The headers on overlays, popups, and dialogs—such as edit and create windows or windows that open from actions in the action bar—aren't affected by this setting. These headers are always white, to provide a visual indicator that the user is performing an action as opposed to simply viewing information.
Loading Page Color	The background color on the loading page that appears after a mobile user logs in.
Loading Page Logo	The image on the loading page that appears after a mobile user logs in.
	We recommend using an image with the largest dimensions allowable for best results. Maximum image size is 460 pixels by 560 pixels.

You can also customize the branding for the Salesforce1 app login page. My Domain must be enabled to modify the login page. To customize your company's Salesforce1 login page, see "Customize Your Login Page Branding" in the Salesforce Help.

Tips for Branding Your Salesforce1 App

If you're thinking about rebranding the Salesforce1 app, here are some tips to keep in mind.

- When considering color schemes, fonts, and other branding changes, refer to the *Salesforce1 Style Guide*.
- When creating your logo image, be sure to compress it. In many image editing programs, this process is identified as "use compression," "optimize image," "save for web," or "shrink for the web."
- Verify that your logo appears correctly in Salesforce1, using the same devices as your user base, not just a desktop monitor. Your image can render at different scales or proportions depending on the screen size and pixel density of each device.
- Salesforce1 supports `.png`, `.gif`, and `.jpg` image formats for custom branding elements, but we recommend using .png for the best results.
- These interface elements can't be customized:
  - The Salesforce1 app icon that appears on the mobile device's home screen.
  - The initial loading screen when launching the Salesforce1 downloadable app for iOS. This loading screen appears before the user is prompted by the login page.
- Your mobile users must close the app and then log in again to see any custom branding changes.

CHAPTER 8   Learning More

If you want to explore more of what you can do with Salesforce1, these resources can help.

Salesforce1 Rollout Guide

After you've configured your organization and customized it for Salesforce1, it's time to roll out the Salesforce1 mobile apps to your users. Visit this site to see Salesforce's five steps to a successful rollout.

Salesforce1 App Developer Guide

A composite book with both administrator and developer content that walks you through Salesforce1 using a series of tutorials with sample data in a Developer organization. Includes chapters on page layouts, compact layouts, actions, Salesforce1 customization, Visualforce, canvas apps, and custom actions.

Trailhead Module: Salesforce1 Mobile Basics

A fun, interactive way to learn about Salesforce1 in a browser by walking through exercises in a Developer Edition organization, taking challenges, and earning badges.

Salesforce Help & Training Portal

A site devoted to the help documentation for Salesforce. Get help for what you're working on, find answers to your questions, and download tip sheets and other guides.

Salesforce Success Community

Home to a set of extremely useful tools to help you get your Salesforce work done. Connect with Salesforce customers, partners, product specialists and employees to learn, get answers to your questions, and share new ideas.

CHAPTER 9   Appendices

One of the goals of this guide is to help you, as an administrator, navigate the sometimes complex world of Salesforce1. In these appendices, we've included some extra material that we hope you'll find useful, including edition and license information, a chart outlining the feature support differences between the Salesforce1 downloadable apps and mobile browser app, and more.

How Actions Are Ordered in the Salesforce1 Action Bar and List Item Actions

The Salesforce1 and Lightning Experience Actions section of a page layout and global publisher layout drives which actions appear in Salesforce1. It also enables you to customize the order of quick actions, productivity actions, and standard and custom buttons that are available as actions.

If you customize the Salesforce1 and Lightning Experience Actions section of a layout, Salesforce1 reflects your customizations.

If you customize the actions in the Quick Actions in the Salesforce Classic Publisher section, but don't customize the action bar section, the Salesforce1 action bar inherits its quick actions from the Quick Actions in the Salesforce Classic Publisher section.

If neither section is customized, the action bar inherits a default set of actions predefined by Salesforce. The sets of actions differ between objects, based on the most common or typical activities required for each object.

How Predefined Actions Are Ordered in the Salesforce1 Action Bar and List Item Actions

Your organization's page layouts and publisher layouts control the order in which actions appear in the Salesforce1 action bar and list item actions. If you don't customize the actions in the action bar on a page layout or global publisher layout, the location of key actions is predefined by Salesforce.

🛈 **Important:** This predefined ordering chart applies only if you *haven't* customized the Salesforce1 and Lightning Experience Actions section of an object's page layout or on a global publisher layout.

If you haven't customized the Salesforce1 action bar, the quick actions in the predefined set are derived from the actions in the "Quick Actions in the Salesforce Classic Publisher" section of the associated object page layout or global publisher layout.

On object page layouts, when the Salesforce1 action bar isn't customized:
   If the Quick Actions in the Salesforce Classic Publisher section is customized, the quick actions in the action bar inherit those customizations.

If neither section is customized, the quick actions in the action bar are inherited from the Quick Actions in the Salesforce Classic Publisher section of the global publisher layout.

On global publisher layouts, when the Salesforce1 action bar isn't customized:

If the Quick Actions in the Salesforce Classic Publisher section is customized, the quick actions in the action bar inherit those customizations.

If neither section is customized, the quick actions in the action bar for global pages default to a Salesforce predefined set.

The predefined actions in the action bar, list item actions, and associated action menus are divided into groups. The arrangement of these groups is fixed, but the order of actions within the groups can vary based on the object and the actions that are present on the global publisher layout or on an object's page layout. Not every object or page displays every group.

Here's the breakdown of which actions are contained in each group for each object or page.

Object or Page	Action Group 1	Action Group 2	Action Group 3	Action Group 4	Action Group 5	Action Group 6
Account	1. Call, 2. New Task, 3. New Event, 4. Post	5. Edit	Remaining quick actions from the Quick Actions in the Salesforce Classic Publisher section. If that section isn't customized, remaining quick actions are inherited from the Quick Actions in the Salesforce Classic Publisher	Custom buttons that are supported in Salesforce1, in the order defined on the page layout.*	Remaining standard buttons that are supported in Salesforce1, in the order defined on the page layout.	View Website (if the `Website` field is populated)

Object or Page	Action Group 1	Action Group 2	Action Group 3	Action Group 4	Action Group 5	Action Group 6
			section of the *global publisher layout*.			
Case	First three quick actions in the order defined on the page layout, 4. Post	5. Edit	Remaining quick actions from the Quick Actions in the Salesforce Classic Publisher section. If that section isn't customized, remaining quick actions are inherited from the Quick Actions in the Salesforce Classic Publisher section of the *global publisher layout*.	Custom buttons that are supported in Salesforce1, in the order defined on the page layout.*	Remaining standard buttons that are supported in Salesforce1, in the order defined on the page layout.	
Contact	1. Call, 2. New Task, 3. New Event	4. Edit	Remaining quick actions from the Quick Actions in	Custom buttons that are supported in Salesforce1,	Remaining standard buttons that are supported in	

Object or Page	Action Group 1	Action Group 2	Action Group 3	Action Group 4	Action Group 5	Action Group 6
			the Salesforce Classic Publisher section. If that section isn't customized, remaining quick actions are inherited from the Quick Actions in the Salesforce Classic Publisher section of the *global publisher layout.*	in the order defined on the page layout.*	Salesforce1, in the order defined on the page layout.	
Custom Object	First four actions in the order defined on the page layout	5. Edit	Remaining quick actions from the Quick Actions in the Salesforce Classic Publisher section. If that section isn't customized, remaining	Custom buttons that are supported in Salesforce1, in the order defined on the page layout.*	Remaining standard buttons that are supported in Salesforce1, in the order defined on the page layout.	

Object or Page	Action Group 1	Action Group 2	Action Group 3	Action Group 4	Action Group 5	Action Group 6
			quick actions are inherited from the Quick Actions in the Salesforce Classic Publisher section of the *global publisher layout*.			
Event	Quick actions in the order defined on the layout. Standard Chatter actions aren't supported.	Edit, Delete				
Feed	Quick actions in the order defined on the global publisher layout					
Group	First four actions in the order defined on the global publisher layout	Remaining quick actions in the order defined on the global publisher layout	Edit	Leave Group		

Object or Page	Action Group 1	Action Group 2	Action Group 3	Action Group 4	Action Group 5	Action Group 6
Lead	1. Log a Call, 2. New Task, 3. Convert (if enabled), 4. Post	4. Edit	Remaining quick actions from the Quick Actions in the Salesforce Classic Publisher section. If that section isn't customized, remaining quick actions are inherited from the Quick Actions in the Salesforce Classic Publisher section of the *global publisher layout*.	Custom buttons that are supported in Salesforce1, in the order defined on the page layout.*	Remaining standard buttons that are supported in Salesforce1, in the order defined on the page layout.	Call, Send Email
Lightning Page	Actions in the order defined in the Lightning Page					
List View	1. Filter, 2. Sort, 3. New					

Object or Page	Action Group 1	Action Group 2	Action Group 3	Action Group 4	Action Group 5	Action Group 6
Object Home Page (Tablet Only)	1. New, 2. Sort					
Opportunity	1. Log a Call, 2. New Task, 3. New Event, 4. Post	5. Edit	Remaining quick actions from the Quick Actions in the Salesforce Classic Publisher section. If that section isn't customized, remaining quick actions are inherited from the Quick Actions in the Salesforce Classic Publisher section of the *global publisher layout*.	Custom buttons that are supported in Salesforce1, in the order defined on the page layout.*	Remaining standard buttons that are supported in Salesforce1, in the order defined on the page layout.	
People	1. Call, 2. Send Email, 3. Post	4. Edit	Remaining actions in the order defined on the global	Custom buttons that are supported in Salesforce1, in the order	Remaining standard buttons that are supported in Salesforce1,	

Object or Page	Action Group 1	Action Group 2	Action Group 3	Action Group 4	Action Group 5	Action Group 6
			publisher layout	defined on the page layout.*	in the order defined on the page layout.	
Person Account	1. Call, 2. Send Email, 3. New Task, 4. New Event	5. Edit	Remaining quick actions from the Quick Actions in the Salesforce Classic Publisher section. If that section isn't customized, remaining quick actions are inherited from the Quick Actions in the Salesforce Classic Publisher section of the *global publisher layout*.	Custom buttons that are supported in Salesforce1, in the order defined on the page layout.*	Remaining standard buttons that are supported in Salesforce1, in the order defined on the page layout.	Map, Read News, View Website
Related List (for standard objects)	1. New					

Object or Page	Action Group 1	Action Group 2	Action Group 3	Action Group 4	Action Group 5	Action Group 6
Search Results	1. New, 2. Sort					
Salesforce Today—Main Page	Quick actions in the order defined on the global publisher layout					
Salesforce Today—Mobile Calendar Event	1. Quick Message, 2. Join Conference Call, 3. Map		Remaining quick actions from the Quick Actions in the Salesforce Classic Publisher section. If that section isn't customized, remaining quick actions are inherited from the Quick Actions in the Salesforce Classic Publisher section of the *global publisher layout*.			

Object or Page	Action Group 1	Action Group 2	Action Group 3	Action Group 4	Action Group 5	Action Group 6
Task	1. Edit Comments, 2. Change Date, 3. Change Status, 4. Change Priority	5. Edit	Remaining quick actions from the Quick Actions in the Salesforce Classic Publisher section. If that section isn't customized, remaining quick actions are inherited from the Quick Actions in the Salesforce Classic Publisher section of the *global publisher layout*. Standard Chatter actions aren't supported.	Custom buttons that are supported in Salesforce1, in the order defined on the page layout.[*]	Remaining standard buttons that are supported in Salesforce1, in the order defined on the page layout.	

As we mentioned, some actions are in fixed positions. In places where you see a numbered list in the table, this is the fixed order that those actions appear in on the action bar, list item actions, and in the respective action menus.

For example, for the Account object, the standard Chatter Post action is in the fourth position. This is fixed. Regardless of where you put the Post action in the account page layout, Post always displays in the fourth position.

However, deletion of actions is always respected. So in our example, if you delete the Post action from the account page layout, the remaining actions move up and you see Edit in the fourth position.

* Custom buttons that are added to the Button section of a page layout and that use a Visualforce page as the content source are supported in Salesforce1. Remember that the Visualforce page must be enabled for use in Salesforce1. Custom links, custom buttons that are added to list views, and custom buttons that define the content source as `URL` or `OnClick JavaScript` aren't available in Salesforce1.

Actions with and without Chatter

Use actions regardless of whether Chatter or actions in the publisher are enabled.

The actions that are available in the full Salesforce site or in Salesforce1 To enable or disable Chatter for your organization, from Setup, enter `Chatter Settings` in the `Quick Find` box, then select **Chatter Settings**. If Chatter is enabled, the `Enable Actions in the Publisher` option controls whether the actions that you create display in the Chatter publisher.

EDITIONS

Available in: Salesforce Classic and Lightning Experience

Quick actions available in: **Group, Professional, Enterprise, Performance, Unlimited, Contact Manager, Database.com,** and **Developer** Editions

Custom canvas actions available in: **Professional** (with Force.com Canvas enabled), **Enterprise, Performance, Unlimited,** and **Developer** Editions

	Chatter Off, Actions Off	Chatter On, Actions Off	Chatter On, Actions On
You can create global actions and customize global action lists	Yes	Yes	Yes
You can create object-specific actions and customize object-specific action lists	Yes	Yes	Yes
Actions appear on the Home page and Chatter home	No	Yes[1]	Yes

	Chatter Off, Actions Off	Chatter On, Actions Off	Chatter On, Actions On
page in the full Salesforce site			
Actions appear in object feeds in the full Salesforce site	No	Yes[1,2]	Yes[2]
The action bar is available in the Salesforce1 feed	No[3]	Yes[4]	Yes
The action bar is available on the record view in Salesforce1	Yes[5]	Yes[6]	Yes[6]
The action bar is available on Lightning Pages in Salesforce1	Yes[5]	Yes	Yes

Footnotes:

1. If actions in the publisher aren't enabled, only standard Chatter actions (Post, File, Link, Poll, and Thanks) appear in the Chatter publisher in the full Salesforce site.

2. The Chatter feed appears on an object's detail page in the full Salesforce site only for objects that have feed tracking enabled.

3. When Chatter is disabled, the Feed item isn't available in Salesforce1.

4. When Chatter is enabled but actions in the publisher aren't, standard Chatter actions and nonstandard actions appear in the Salesforce1 action bar and in third-party apps that use action lists. Nonstandard actions include Create, Update, Log a Call, custom actions, and Mobile Smart Actions.

5. When Chatter and actions in the publisher are disabled, only nonstandard actions appear in the action bar in Salesforce1 or in third-party apps that use action lists. Nonstandard actions include Create, Update, Log a Call, custom actions, and Mobile Smart Actions.

6. If feed tracking isn't enabled on the object, only nonstandard actions appear in the Salesforce1 action bar and in third-party apps that use action lists. Nonstandard actions include Create, Update, Log a Call, custom actions, and Mobile Smart Actions.

Salesforce1 Mobile App Features: What's Available in Each Version

Salesforce1 is available as a downloadable app on iOS and Android devices, as well as browser-based app. In most cases the downloadable and mobile browser apps include the same features. But there are some differences between the experiences, often related to differences in the mobile platforms on which Salesforce1 is supported.

Feature	iOS and Android Downloadable Apps (v7.x)	Mobile Browser App
Navigation and Actions		
Access up to 200 list views per object	✔	✔
See visual snapshots of business data on list view charts		✔ *(tablets only)*
Sort and filter list views	✔	✔
Do actions like make phone calls, log calls, send emails, map locations, and view news or Websites *(Phone calls supported on iPhones and Android phones only)*	✔	✔
Use quick actions created for your organization	✔	✔
Search		
Search for Salesforce records	✔	✔
Scope global searches to find records by object		✔
See matching search results for all records, not just those that have been recently viewed		✔
Sort search results		✔
Relationship and Data Management		
Add new records and update existing records	✔	✔
Prevent the creation of duplicate records	✔	✔

Feature	iOS and Android Downloadable Apps (v7.x)	Mobile Browser App
Add contacts to Salesforce from mobile device contact lists	✔	
Locate, associate, and view Twitter profiles for Salesforce accounts, contacts, and leads	✔	✔
Work with data stored outside of Salesforce	✔ *(iOS only)*	✔
Sales Productivity		
Take rich text meeting notes and easily relate them to records	✔	✔
Track the latest news about accounts	✔	✔
Convert qualified leads to contacts	✔	✔
Use Sales Path to follow sales processes and get deals closed	✔	✔
Salesforce Today and Activities		
Use Today to prepare for and manage the day's events, join conference calls, and log mobile calendar events in Salesforce	✔	
Add contacts to Salesforce from events in Today	✔	
Create tasks from Chatter posts		✔
Create tasks from Notes	✔	✔
Track, close, or reopen tasks	✔	✔
Do quick task updates with a tap: edit comments or change a due date, status, or priority	✔	✔
Create and view Salesforce events	✔	✔
Work.com		
Use Work.com Coaching, Goals, Rewards, and Skills	✔ *(Skills in Android only)*	✔

Feature	iOS and Android Downloadable Apps (v7.x)	Mobile Browser App
Customer Service Tools		
Use Social Customer Service to track cases and respond to Twitter Tweets in real time	✔	✔
View Salesforce Knowledge articles		✔
Salesforce1 Reporting		
View dashboards, dashboard components (including Visualforce dashboard components), and reports	✔	✔
Sort data in reports	✔	✔
Apply dashboard filters	✔	✔
Share dashboards in feeds	✔ *(iOS only, limited)*	✔
Chatter (Feeds, Profiles, Groups, Files		
Use Chatter feeds, people, and groups	✔	✔
Search in the main Chatter feed	✔	✔
View, edit, and follow feed entries organized by topic; add multiple topics to posts		✔
Bundle multiple record updates into a single post		✔
Attach photos or files to posts or comments, or use quick actions to post photos or files	✔	✔
Share Chatter posts	✔	
See previews of files posted to posts and comments	✔	✔
Double-tap to add or remove bookmarks for Chatter posts	✔	
Ask questions and get answers in the feed		✔
Escalate questions in Chatter to cases		✔

Feature	iOS and Android Downloadable Apps (v7.x)	Mobile Browser App
Edit user profile details	✔ *(Android only)*	✔
Change the user profile picture	✔	✔
Add records to groups	✔	✔
Collaborate with more privacy in unlisted Chatter groups	✔	✔
Post announcements in group feeds	✔	✔
Manage groups	✔	✔
Use Salesforce Files *(Requires Chatter)*	✔	✔
Browse and share files from external data sources, such as SharePoint or OneDrive for Business *(Requires Files Connect)*		✔
Use Salesforce1 if Chatter is turned off	✔	✔
Use quick actions in Salesforce1 if Chatter is turned off	✔	✔
Launch Salesforce1 from Chatter email notifications and digest links	✔	✔
Business Logic and Process Automation		
Submit records for approval	✔	✔
View the status of pending approvals and approve or reject approval requests	✔ *(iOS only)*	✔
Resume or delete paused flow interviews		✔
Notifications		
Receive in-app notifications	✔	✔
Receive push notifications	✔	
Configure the push notifications that are sent	✔	

Feature	iOS and Android Downloadable Apps (v7.x)	Mobile Browser App
Offline		
View cached data when working offline	✔	
Access		
Access communities created using the Salesforce Tabs + Visualforce template	✔	✔
Switch between multiple Salesforce accounts or communities without leaving the app	✔	
Open most Salesforce URLs directly in Salesforce1	✔ *(iOS only)*	
Configure connections to multiple instances from the login page	✔	
Control app access with a security PIN	✔	
Customizations and User/App Settings		
View Visualforce pages	✔	✔
Access Lightning pages, and custom and third-party apps	✔	✔
See a customized selection and arrangement of actions in the action bar and list item actions	✔	✔
See custom branding	✔	✔

Salesforce1 Editions and Licenses

These Salesforce editions and user license types allow the use of Salesforce1.

Salesforce Editions		
These Salesforce editions allow the use of Salesforce1.	• Personal Edition	Database.com Edition isn't supported.

- Group Edition
- Professional Edition
- Enterprise Edition
- Performance Edition
- Unlimited Edition
- Developer Edition
- Contact Manager Edition

User License Types

These user license types can access Salesforce1. A special Salesforce1 or mobile license isn't required.

- Salesforce users
- Salesforce Platform and Force.com users
- Chatter Plus users (also known as Chatter Only), Chatter Free users, and Chatter External users[*]
- Customer Community, Customer Community Plus, and Partner Community external users
- Portal users who are a member of a Salesforce community

These user license types aren't supported: portal users (unless a member of a Salesforce community), Database.com users, Sites and Site.com users, Data.com users, and Work.com users.

INDEX

Index

Notes

Notes

Notes

Notes

Notes

Notes

Notes

Notes

Notes

Notes

Notes

Notes

Notes

Notes

Notes

Notes

Notes

Notes

Notes

Notes